Dedication

To the quiet moments behind closed
doors, where breath slows,
thoughts settle and the world waits.

To the loo, that humble sanctuary of release,
reflection and, occasionally, revelation.

May this book help you let go of more
than just yesterday's regrets…
and that questionable hummus.

First published in 2025 by Allsorted
WD19 4BG UK

The authorised representative in the EU is
Petit Pop Agencies, Unit 8 Robinhood Business Park, Robinhood Road, Dublin 22, D22 A370, Ireland
email: info@petitpop.com
www.saturdaypublishing.com

Copyright © 2025 Saturday Publishing

All rights reserved. No part of this publication may be reproduced or transmitted in any form or by any means, electronic, or mechanical, including photocopying, recording, or by any information storage and retrieval system, without permission in writing from the publisher.

ISBN 9781917535243

Written and designed by Emily Snape

DISCLAIMER

Sacred Legal Aura Activation: While my cosmic colon-clearing insights are nearly miraculous, they are strictly for amusement. Please consult an earthly health-care professional before attempting any throne-based enlightenment.

The Power of Letting One Go

ALLSORTED.

Contents

Chapter 1 – Page 9
The Breath of Release

Core Principle
Breath is the gateway between chaos
and calm – even in close quarters.

Your Practice
Learn to breathe with majesty,
intention and strategic nostril control.

Chapter 2 – Page 41
The Sacred Act of Sitting

Core Principle
Grounded posture is a form of power,
even with your trousers down.

Your Practice
Sit with presence, poise and the
quiet confidence of a Zen loo lord.

Chapter 3 – Page 65
The Art of Letting Go

Core Principle
True freedom comes from release:
physical, emotional, ancestral.

Your Practice
Embrace surrender, forgive your past
and flush like you mean it.

Chapter 4 – Page 85
The Mirror of the Moment

Core Principle
Reflection begins in stillness (and possibly while scrolling).

Your Practice
Observe, laugh, cringe and
emerge wiser, cleaner and more you.

Chapter 5 – Page 95
The Ripple Effect

Core Principle
What happens on the throne doesn't stay on the throne.

Your Practice
Carry your porcelain wisdom into the wild.

Close your eyes.
You are entering the
sacred chamber of release,
where the body surrenders
and the soul ascends.

Chapter 1

The Breath of Release

The bathroom is not just a room.
It is a portal. A sacred space where the
boundaries between the physical and the
metaphysical dissolve.

In this chapter, we shall explore the
ancient, universal power of breath. An act
so profound, so transformative, that it has
been practised by every living being
since time immemorial.

Prepare to transcend.

When your mind spirals into how someone's dog has a better life than you… inhale. Exhale. You are not behind, just buffering.

Exercise One

The Breath of Infinite Majesty

You are not merely sitting.
You are ascending.

While others see four walls and a lock that barely works, you recognize the truth: this is your throne. A ceramic altar. A sacred chamber where kings, queens and constipated mystics alike have communed with the divine.

This breathwork practice is for the moments when you need to remember who you are.

Not just a person with a body, but a vessel of radiant power – seated nobly upon your very own plinth (plumbing optional).

Exercise One

1.
Take your seat with quiet dignity. Allow your spine to lengthen upward, as if gently drawn toward the sky. Imagine a soft crown of light resting atop your head – a symbol of awareness and inner poise.

2.
Inhale slowly and deeply through your nose for a count of four. Breathe in not just air, but clarity, stillness and presence. If the air carries traces of your recent… release, simply acknowledge it without judgement. Even nature has its fragrance.

3.
Hold your breath for a count of two. In this pause, feel the subtle energy within your body begin to move. Picture it swirling gently through you, like a cleansing wind in a quiet room. Preferably one with decent ventilation.

Exercise One

4.
Exhale smoothly through your mouth for a count of six. Let this breath carry away tension, distraction and anything that no longer serves you, both physically and emotionally.

Repeat five times.

With each cycle, sense your inner space expanding. This is not merely a pause in your day; it is a return to the calm centre of your being.

Note
The bathroom may be humble, but within these walls great awakenings are possible. Just remember to crack open a window if enlightenment begins to smell a bit too human.

If the cost of
life triggers an
existential wobble,
return to the breath.
Inner calm is still free.
For now.

Exercise Two

The Rhythmic Breath of Galactic Harmony

Even in the most earthly of settings,
you are part of something vast.

This practice invites you to steady your breath, quiet your mind and sync yourself with the gentle rhythm of the cosmos – whether that's your inner universe or just the echo of a leaky tap.

Exercise Two

1.
Inhale slowly through your nose for a count of four. Visualize the breath as silvery stardust, drifting down into your lungs, settling like moonlight on a still pond.

2.
Hold the breath for two. In this suspended moment, sense the silence between the stars, the stillness that holds it all together. That same stillness lives within you, right between your ribs and just above the curry you had last night.

3.
Exhale gently through your mouth for six counts. Let the breath carry away worries, urgency, to-do lists and anything else you accidentally brought in with you.

Exercise Two

4.
Repeat this cycle until your inner chaos is tidied up like a well-folded duvet and your nervous system is purring like a contented cat floating through space.

Optional Mantra (murmured like a BBC nature documentary narrator):

"I am calm. I am vast.
I am slightly echoey in here."

Note
If your Wi-Fi signal improves during this exercise, take full credit. If it doesn't, at least your chakras are buffering beautifully.

Visualize your burdens
dissolving like organic
gluten-free soap
in ethically sourced
rainwater.

Exercise Three

The Cosmic Flush Visualization

This moment may appear mundane,
but it holds quiet power.

Within these walls, you enter a space of surrender – a pause where the clutter of the mind and the weight of the day can be gently cleared.

Each breath becomes an offering, each exhale a soft unravelling of what you no longer need, from the surface of your thoughts to the
hidden corners of your spirit.

Exercise Three

1.

Close your eyes and take a slow, deliberate breath in through your nose. Let it be ceremonial, as if drawing in the wisdom of the universe or, at the very least, the air just above the zone of… atmospheric compromise.

2.

As you exhale, visualize your burdens – worries, guilt, old grudges, that thing you said in Year 9 – swirling into a golden spiral. See them descending, like leaves caught in a gentle whirlpool, drawn down into the unseen depths.

3.

With each breath, feel yourself becoming lighter, clearer and more at ease. Allow your thoughts to settle like dust in sunlight. There is no need to hold on. Even gravity is on your side.

Exercise Three

4.

When you are ready, open your eyes. Reach for the handle, and flush with intention. Not just the physical but the emotional, the ancestral, the energetic. Yes, even the family drama.

Let it go. All of it.

Optional Mantra (whispered with grace):

"Down it goes, and so do I rise."

Note
If the flush doesn't take the first time, don't be discouraged.

Even spiritual release can require a second go.

If your bank says "declined" but your soul says "aligned", trust your soul. The universe accepts all forms of credit – eventually.

Exercise Four

The Whispering Teacup Breath

This breath practice invites stillness in the way only a bathroom can: quiet, tiled and out of reach from group chats and doorbell deliveries.

It's about the soft pause… the moment before a flush, a thought or a poorly timed question through the door.

Exercise Four

1.
Sit comfortably, ideally on the porcelain throne. Let your shoulders drop like a towel from a heated rail.

2.
Inhale gently through your nose for a count of three, as though sipping the steam off a hot cup of tea that you absolutely shouldn't have brought into the loo but did anyway.

3.
Pause.
Not a dramatic hold, just a gentle hover.

The kind of breath you'd take before saying something clever… or checking if anyone forgot to replace the toilet roll.

Exercise Four

4.
Exhale slowly through your
mouth for a count of five.

Let it out like a sigh of relief
after just making it in time.

Repeat five times
(or until someone tries the door
handle and ruins your spiritual flow).

Note
For best results, aim to match your
breath with the gentle hum of the extractor fan.

If you haven't got one, your own
gentle wheezing will do.

True greatness isn't about what you're doing… it's about sitting still, breathing deeply and resisting the urge to wonder what's for dinner.

Exercise Five

The Breath of Grateful Release

Gratitude and bowel movements share a secret truth: both feel better when you're fully present.

This exercise invites you to appreciate not just what you have, but where you are… right here, in the only room where you can say "I need a minute" and actually mean it.

Exercise Five

1.
Place one hand on your stomach and
the other wherever feels natural
(armrest, knee, spare loo roll).

2.
Inhale for four counts, and think of something –
anything – you're grateful for. A quiet moment. A
working flush. A seat that's not cold. Little wins.

3.
Hold that breath for two. Let the good feeling
settle in like a cat on your lap –
or a particularly committed poo.

4.
Exhale slowly for six counts, releasing any
pressure, physical or mental. Let the breath carry
away expectations, comparison and the idea that
this moment needs to be anything
other than what it is.

Exercise Five

Repeat until you're filled with warmth, lightness and perhaps a strange sense of toilet-based joy.

Optional Mantra:

"Thank you, loo. Thank you, me.
Thank you, bran cereal."

Note
This may be the only place in your life where you're not expected to multitask.
Enjoy it. Deeply.

Before we plunge into the next wave
of inner release, take a moment.

Not every great journey is one of effort.

Some are just… sitting and thinking.

Il-loo-minating Self-Inquiry

What am I still holding on to that no longer needs to be part of me?

If I flushed my fears, what space would that make inside me?

Who would I be if I stopped trying so hard and just… sat?

Have I mistaken urgency for purpose?

Is it time to stop scrolling and start wiping the slate clean?

Loo Yoga

The Porcelain Pretzel

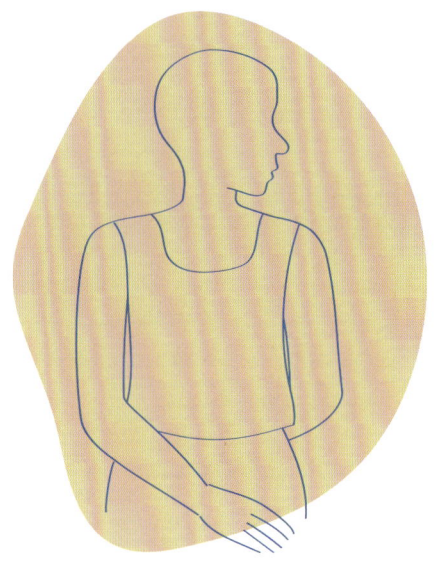

While seated comfortably (you already are),
gently turn your upper body to the left, letting
your right hand rest on your left thigh. Hold for
a few breaths. Then swap sides.
Twist out tension. Realign your back.
Just… mind your balance.

The TP Reach

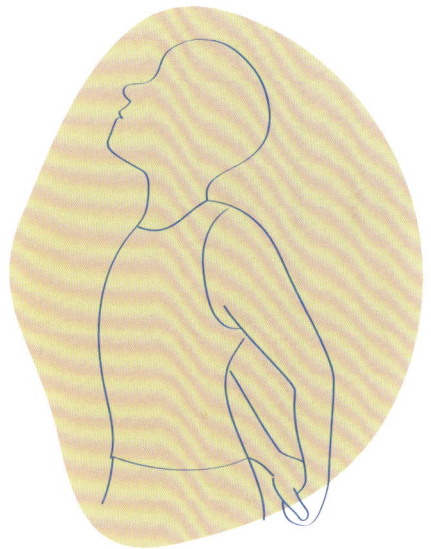

Place your hands behind your back and clasp them together. Gently lift your chest. This opens the heart and reminds you that, sometimes, what you need is just slightly out of reach.

Like the spare roll under the sink.

Moments of Micro-Enlightenment

A checklist of quiet awakenings experienced during your most private seated retreat.

- ☐ Genuinely forgave someone… until you remember what they said in 2014

- ☐ Let go of needing to be productive – for a full seven minutes

- ☐ Felt strangely moved by the way the light hit the bathroom tiles

- ☐ Realized your body knows how to let go – even when your mind doesn't

- ☐ Understood that not replying to a message is a form of self-respect

- ☐ Embraced stillness without checking the time (twice)

- ☐ Released tension, expectation and possibly something else

- ☐ Remembered you're not behind – you're just on a scenic route

- ☐ Briefly felt like the Dalai Lama… then reached for the air freshener

- ☐ Solved a life dilemma without Googling it

Optional Reflection:

You don't need to tick every box. One tiny shift in posture or thought can echo through your whole day.

Chapter 2

The Sacred Act of Sitting

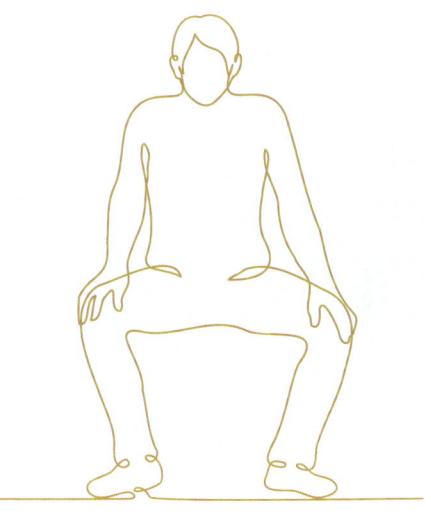

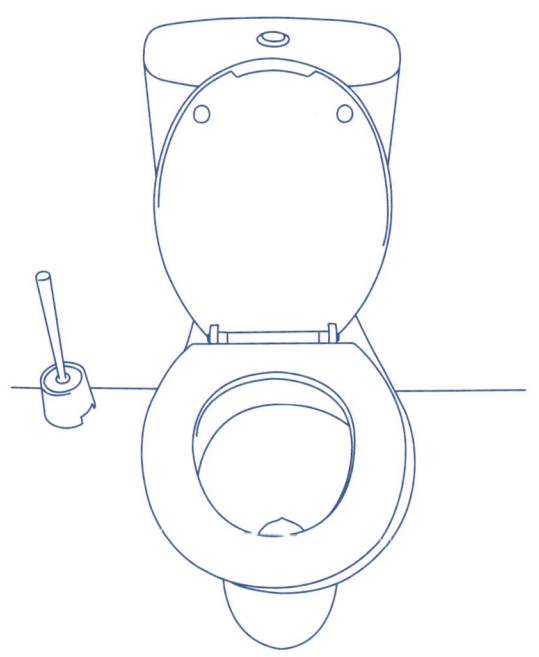

While some may see sitting as
passive, you know better.

This is a practice of presence. A bold act
of surrender. A commitment to being still
while the world spins madly
beyond the door.

Whether you're perching, balancing or
settling in like a meditating buddha on
a bidet, sitting is the gateway to insight,
serenity and, occasionally, numb thighs.

Assume position.
Not for duty –
for dignity.
The throne
demands
nothing.

Exercise One

The Throne Pose of Supreme Stillness

Assume your rightful place.

This is not just a seat. It is *the* seat.
A pedestal of possibility. A sanctuary of stillness.
Here, behind closed doors, the world fades.
Time bends. You are no longer in a rush. You
are a stone in a stream. Unmoved. Unbothered.
Borderline majestic. Let your spine lengthen like
a proud flagpole on the high seas. Let your face
soften. Let your thoughts idle in neutral.

This is not the time for doing.
This is the sacred act of sitting.
Breathe. Be. Don't check your phone.
(Okay, maybe just once.)

Exercise One

1.
Gently lower yourself into position. No plonking. Ease down like you're being lowered by invisible ropes of destiny. Nobility never crashes.

2.
Let your hands rest naturally on your knees, in your lap, or loosely cradling your sixth attempt at today's Wordle. This is your time. Your kingdom.

3.
Soften your gaze or close your eyes entirely. Allow your mind to attune to the subtle symphony around you: the hum of distant plumbing, the noble sigh of ventilation, the faint echo of someone else's questionable choices two cubicles over.

4.
Breathe normally. The only movement is the gentle rise and fall of your chest. Let your shoulders melt. Let your jaw unclench.

Exercise One

You are safe. You are steady.
You are seated on a mighty throne.

5.
Remain here for a minute or five. Let time lose
its edges. Your only task is to exist, with quiet
dignity and perhaps a faint draught
on your calves.

Note
Never underestimate the wisdom that arrives
when your trousers are down and
no one's asking you to speak.
Some call it rest. Some call it surrender. You,
seated proudly upon the ceramic summit,
may simply call it: Tuesday.

Sometimes balance isn't found within. It's found when the seat is finally warm and evenly occupied.

Exercise Two

The Mindful Wiggle of Realignment

You've committed to the sit
but are you truly aligned?

The Mindful Wiggle is the ancient art of… well, shuffling. A sacred squirm. It brings awareness to your posture, your seat and that awkward realization that perhaps the lid wasn't fully down. This is not fidgeting. This is realignment with purpose. A gentle recalibration of bottom and bowl. Your throne deserves respect,
and so do your buttocks.

Through the Wiggle, we find balance. Through balance, we find peace. Through peace… we stop feeling that one weird pressure point.

Exercise Two

1.
Begin with a subtle shift side to side. Explore the connection between bum and bowl. Let your sit bones converse with the seat beneath. Are you evenly distributed, or spiritually leaning left?

2.
Adjust as needed. Slowly. With dignity. No panicked hops. No frantic rebalancing. Just regal recalibration, like a queen adjusting her crown. (But, you know, further south.)

3.
With each tiny shuffle, visualize your spine stacking like bricks of cosmic awareness. This isn't fidgeting – it's enlightenment… with a touch of cheek.

4.
Rest here. You've earned it. You've conquered the wobble. You are centred. You are still. You are seated in full sphinctral harmony.

Exercise Two

Note
If your toilet seat creaks loudly during this, consider it applause from the universe. If it cracks… well, that's still feedback. Honour it.

Why book a retreat when wisdom arrives mid-squat? A slight lean back offers clarity, without the hefty price tag or mandatory kombucha.

Exercise Three

The Gentle Hinge of Contemplation

Many great thoughts were born in the bathroom, hunched slightly forward, trousers round ankles, pondering life like a philosopher in resplendent robes.

This micro-movement invites insight without the neck strain. A slight tilt backward brings clarity, without forcing you into an awkward, crumpled heap.

Relaxation and wisdom don't need to be painful – they just need a gentle nudge.

Exercise Three

1.
Begin seated, with your spine long and straight, as if a delicate string is pulling you upright from the top of your head. You are royalty in repose – don't forget that.

2.
Slowly begin to lean back, but not too far. Think of it like easing into a plush armchair with dignity – no need to lunge back like you're falling into a beanbag. A slight lean will do. You're not just sitting; you're reclining with purpose.

3.
Let your shoulders soften, releasing any tension you didn't even know you were holding. Open your chest gently, like you're about to give a TED talk but don't feel the need to shout.

4.
Your feet must remain grounded, your spine still long and proud. Breathe deeply, with a steady

rhythm. If you hear a soft creak beneath
you, that's just the toilet's way of
applauding your grace.

5.
Take a moment. Sink into the stillness. You're
not just sitting; you're contemplating. You are a
sage, a philosopher, an enlightened soul… or at
the very least, your posture says so.

Note
If your lean shifts a bit too far, and you feel
a wobble, don't panic. Consider it a sign
that you're really sinking into the moment.
Sometimes, the greatest revelations come when
we're a little off balance. Let go of perfection;
embrace the wobble – it's the universe reminding
you that growth often feels a bit unsteady.

Before we embark on the next chapter of release, let's take a moment to appreciate the art of sitting still. Allow your thoughts to marinate in peace. You've just journeyed through a profound moment of inner work – now, relish the calm and quiet, for it is in these moments true transformation takes root. Think of this as your soul's intermission before it dives into the next act of greatness. Remember, not every moment of growth is a dramatic leap. Sometimes, it's just sitting, breathing and waiting for the universe to hand you the next plot twist.

Reflections from the Quiet Cubicle

Some thoughts arrive only in tiled silence:

What if the bathroom isn't an escape, but a return?

Am I here to let go, or to remember who I am when no one's asking for anything?

Does enlightenment flush clockwise or anti-clockwise? (Depends on the hemisphere. And the plumbing.)

Whisperables for the Weary

*Repeat these in your head.
Or whisper, if you're feeling brave and live alone:*

"Release is progress."

"I do not chase. I sit, and it comes."

"I am here, and I am enough.
More than enough, judging by the smell."

Gentle Koans from the Lavatorial Path

*Answers not required.
Only deep, unblinking contemplation.*

If no one knocks for ten full minutes,
have you truly disappeared?

Which is cleaner: an empty mind
or a freshly bleached rim?

When the loo seat is warm…
who was here before you?

Chapter 3

The Art of Letting Go

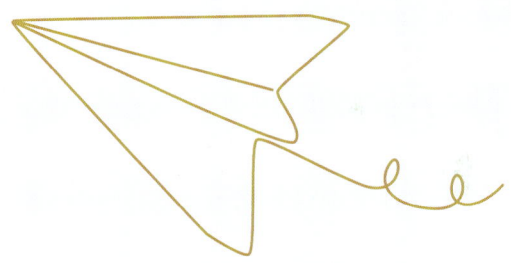

Letting go sounds easy…
But try convincing your mind, which is busy clinging to stress, past mistakes and that one awkward text you sent in 2015. Real freedom comes from releasing, whether it's forgiving the past or just letting go of tension in your shoulders.

Think of it like cleaning out your fridge. You can't make room for the new until you toss the old stuff. Let's get decluttering, so you can finally breathe.

Empowerment comes not in restraint, but in the fearless act of release. Even the humblest of detoxifications can free you of the mightiest burdens.

Exercise One

The Freedom of Flatulence

Sometimes, true freedom isn't found in a calm breath. It's in the release of something more natural. In this exercise, we embrace the most ancient form of release: the fart. Let's call it a gastric awakening, a bodily reminder that freedom comes from surrender.

This isn't just a bodily function; it's a profound act of release. As you let go, allow yourself to shed what no longer serves you – whether that's emotional baggage, mental clutter or the remnants of an overindulgent meal.

Each release creates room for lightness, clarity and the new. So, surrender with grace (and maybe a little sound) and feel the liberation in letting go.

Exercise One

1.
Sit comfortably, as if preparing for an important business meeting (though with a much more relaxed agenda).

2.
Focus on the sensation in your stomach. Notice the tightness. Could be your stress, or maybe it's the beans you had for lunch.

3.
Slowly release the tension in your abdomen. Don't force anything; just let it out naturally. Whether it's a tiny whisper or a glorious rumble, let it flow.

4.
As you release, imagine your worries also slipping away – maybe with a little toot.

Exercise One

Optional Mantras:

"Release the tension, embrace the wind."
"Let go of what no longer serves you…
and what's about to be expelled."
"Breathe in peace, release the sprouts."
"I am a vessel of calm…
and, occasionally, flatulence."
"Exhale with grace, and may your
stomach follow."

Note
If this causes you to chortle, you're doing it right.

You've just expelled more than just air –
you've let go of something unnecessary.

Letting go doesn't have to be a bang. Sometimes, it's just a subtle pffft of freedom.

Exercise Two

The Silent Sigh

Not every release needs to be loud.

Some things, like tension, can be quietly pushed out. This exercise invites you to master the art of silent surrender. Think of it as an internal whoopee cushion – without the noise.

Exercise Two

1.
Sit tall and relaxed, aligning your posture as though you were a dignified figure ready to transcend the trivialities of life. Breathe deeply, but shift your focus away from the breath itself. Instead, concentrate on the internal sensation of release – no sound, just the internal "ahhh" of letting go.

2.
Imagine the pressure building up inside you. This could be the weight of a stressful week, the unresolved tension in your shoulders or maybe the ghost of last night's nacho binge, still lingering and stubbornly clinging to your system.

3.
Now, slowly, let it go. Forget the dramatic eruptions you see in films – this is a more refined affair. Picture it as a soft, almost imperceptible sigh of release, a gentle expulsion of what no longer serves you. This is the fart's more sophisticated cousin, subtle yet undeniably impactful.

Exercise Two

4.
Feel the relief spread through your body, creating space not just physically but mentally as well.

It's like opening a window in a stuffy room – letting out the stale air and inviting in a refreshing breeze.

With each release, the tension slips away, leaving room for clarity and calm.

Note
If you don't feel a little lighter, check that you haven't been holding on to your entire week's stress. Try again.

Letting go isn't an event.
It's just the absence of
tension you barely
noticed leaving.

Exercise Three

The Great Internal Unclenching

True release isn't always loud or dramatic.

Sometimes, it begins quietly – with a single decision to stop gripping so hard.

In this practice, we turn inward, gently locating and loosening the places we've been clenching for years – both physically and otherwise.

Exercise Three

1.
Begin seated, tall but soft, like a wise elder who's seen some things and no longer needs to prove anything. Close your eyes, or lower your gaze like you're about to deliver some profound ancient truth – mainly to yourself.

2.
Scan your body for the hidden clenches. The jaw you've been holding since Tuesday. The shoulders that think they're earrings. The buttocks that have been braced for impact since 2007. There's no judgement here – just awareness.

3.
Now, release one at a time. Drop the shoulders. Unclench the jaw. Breathe out slowly and give your bottom permission to just… be. You might be surprised at how much tension you were storing in your "dignity zone".

Exercise Three

4.

Feel the ripple effect of this release. Your stomach softens. Your mind stops gripping old stories. Even your ankles seem less defensive. Let this be a moment of radical ease. You're not holding anything together. You don't need to.

Optional Mantras:

"Today I choose ease.
And trousers that don't dig in."
"I unclench, therefore I am."
"Let it go, let it flow, let it be
someone else's problem."

Note

If you find yourself re-clenching mid-practice, don't worry. Life has a way of sneaking tension back in. Just notice it, sigh like a poet in a hammock, and gently let it go again. Unclenching is not a one-time event – it's a lifestyle.

Let it be known: you have unclenched.

Not just your body, but the tight grip on all the things you never needed to carry. In a world that glorifies holding it in, you've chosen release.

You shifted, sighed, maybe even squeaked – and made space for ease.

Let this linger: lightness isn't indulgent. It's essential. And sometimes it makes a funny noise on the way out.

Things You Don't Need to Hold Any Longer

A gentle reminder from the seat of self-awareness.

Let go of…

The imaginary argument you keep
winning in your head.

The inbox guilt –
unread emails are not your moral failing.

That weird noise your stomach made in a
meeting – your legend lives on, but it's time
to move forward.

The pressure to optimize every moment
(even this one).

The idea that healing has to look a certain way.
Sometimes it looks like snacks and no trousers.

The myth that everyone else has it together (spoiler: they don't).

The need to fix what simply has to pass.

The habit of tensing your shoulders before you even enter the room.

Any version of yourself that was built only to impress someone else.

A Thought to Sit With

You are not the sum of what you grip tightly.
You are the space created when you begin to let go.

Chapter 4

The Mirror of the Moment

The Sacred Releaser Archetypes

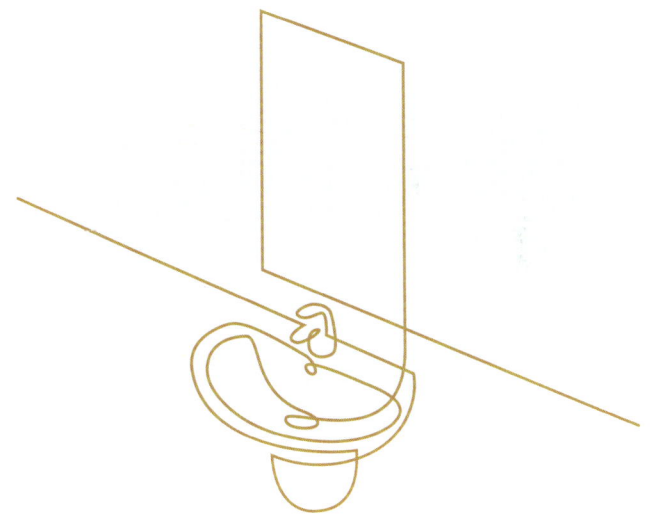

You have journeyed deep into the gentle art of release. But how, dear reader, do you let go? With what style, intention and echo? The time has come to consult the inner oracle of relief. Select your answers carefully. Your archetype awaits.

1.
Upon entering your ceramic sanctum, what is your instinctual approach?

a) You close the door with reverence. This is sacred space.
b) You gather supplies: book, beverage, perhaps a blanket.
c) You sit, then think. Then overthink. Then forget what you came in for.
d) You move fast, close faster, and ensure plausible deniability.

2.
What's your ideal ambient soundtrack
for a moment of release?

a) Complete silence. Anything else would be a violation of ritual.
b) Nature sounds. Possibly a babbling brook, possibly just your pipes.
c) A longform podcast or audiobook you will forget immediately.
d) The extractor fan on full blast. Loud enough to drown guilt.

3.

In the act of release, your guiding principle is:

a) Quiet. Poised. A gentle uncurling of soul and sphincter.
b) Cathartic. Emotional. You may emerge with a new perspective or poem.
c) Unpredictable. You sit for ten minutes, then suddenly solve something cosmic.
d) Tactical. Fast in, fast out. You treat release like a covert op.

4.
What do you most often leave
behind in this space?

a) Nothing but footprints on the bath mat and a faint sense of peace.
b) Thoughts, memories, maybe one tear.
c) Half a theory on time travel and the existential dread of emails.
d) A perfectly neutral atmosphere and zero trace of activity.

Your Archetype, Revealed

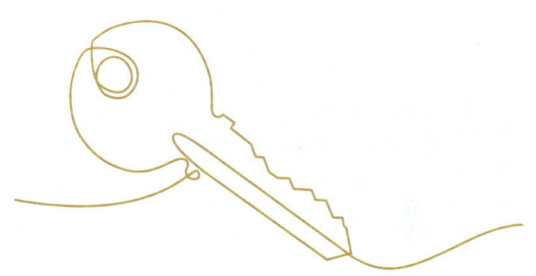

Mostly A's:

The Serene Vessel

You are composed, contemplative and committed to a higher level of toilet-based transcendence. Your bowels move with the phases of the moon. You've likely whispered "I release thee" into the mirror and meant it.

Blessing: May your loo be silent, your soul be light and your candle ever lit.

Mostly B's:

The Emotional Excavator

You do not simply let go – you excavate. A single seated moment can trigger an internal monologue, a Spotify playlist and a profound ancestral unblocking. You feel deeply, flush thoroughly and emerge changed.

Blessing: May your tissues be soft, your exits smooth and your processing complete.

Mostly C's:

The Porcelain Philosopher

You go in for a physical need and emerge with a theory of consciousness. Release is your gateway to insight – awkward, brilliant and often unfinished. Time bends around you. So does your posture.

Blessing: May your wisdom flow freely, your limbs stay numb-free and your revelations stick this time.

Mostly D's:

The Stealth Reliever

Efficiency is your essence. No drama, no witnesses. You are the shadow that leaves no scent. Your talent lies in rapid disconnection and plausible alibis. You may one day write a bestselling guide called *Letting One Go Quietly*.

Blessing: May your hinges be silent, your exits swift and your footsteps masked by ambient sounds.

Chapter 5

The Ripple Effect

We all know the feeling: you've had a profound moment of clarity while seated, your mind free from distractions and your spirit quietly resettling. But now comes the hard part – how to carry that peace, that wisdom, into the "real" world. How to bring that calm and sense of release into your everyday interactions, whether it's a challenging meeting, a chaotic commute or a particularly awkward conversation with a colleague.

This chapter is about taking the freedom you've experienced in your sacred space and letting it ripple outward. You've cleared space physically and emotionally on the throne – now let's do it out there in the world.

The truly free do not march – they saunter, freshly unburdened.

Exercise One

The Post-Throne Zen Walk

Once you've emerged from the tiled temple, reborn and slightly flushed, it's time to take that hard-earned calm into the wild.

This is your victory lap. Walk like someone who's just let go of something heavy – because, spiritually (and maybe literally), you have.

Whether you're striding into a meeting or gliding toward the kettle, let your gait reflect the inner peace of someone who has seen the abyss… and flushed something down it.

Exercise One

1.
Pause before you step out.
Not for dramatic effect (though it helps), but to centre yourself. Take a deep breath. Feel your feet. Remember who you are: a being of light, calmness and recently vacated burdens.

2.
Take your first steps with intention.
Walk slowly. Walk like someone who's read five self-help books but still knows where the biscuits are. Allow your shoulders to drop. Let your hips sway with subtle triumph.

3.
Carry your throne energy.
Don't rush. Glide. You are grace incarnate. Your steps are quiet proclamations of someone who is no longer backed up – emotionally or otherwise.

4.
Smile faintly, like you know something others don't. (Because you do.) You know peace.

Exercise One

You know flow. You know that letting go – privately, peacefully – is a power move.

Optional Mantras:

"I walk in release, not haste."
"Every step is lighter. Every breeze, earned."
"I left something behind. And I don't miss it."
"Let others run. I glide."

Note
If someone asks why you're walking so serenely, simply nod and say, "I've been somewhere." No further details required. Mystery is magnetic. Especially when paired with good posture.

True poise is walking away from nonsense like you've got a secret meeting with the King and a digestive in your pocket.

Exercise Two

The Subtle Art of Strategic Withdrawal

Sometimes, the most powerful move you can make is… absolutely none at all.

After a particularly enlightening bathroom session, the world may seem louder, busier and frankly more annoying than it did five minutes ago.

This exercise is about taking the high road – or at least the quiet exit – when re-entering society.

Exercise Two

1.
Rise with purpose, but not urgency. You are not fleeing the scene. You are gliding into the next chapter of your day.

2.
Walk softly, like someone who's just had a profound experience and is now above small talk. Aim for a knowing half-smile and hands clasped behind your back.

3.
If someone attempts to draw you into chaos (emails, group chats, debates about bins), simply nod with vague wisdom and keep walking. Your silence is your shield.

4.
Settle into your next moment – desk, sofa, snack drawer – with the energy of someone who has seen things and lived to tell the tale, but chooses not to.

Exercise Two

Note
If your re-entry includes socializing, remember: not every thought needs sharing, and not every invitation needs accepting. Your inner peace is allowed to RSVP "no".

After what you've just accomplished in there, a performance review is child's play.

Exercise Three

The Power Walk

You've just conquered the bathroom. Now it's time to take that quiet strength and channel it into your walk. Because let's face it, if you can sit down, get up and leave the throne without having a meltdown, you can handle anything this world throws your way.

This exercise is designed to help you embody that newfound power with every step you take. Whether you're walking to the kettle, commuting to the office or just trying to escape another meeting about "synergy", you'll do it with a purpose – like the majestic gazelle you are.

Exercise Three

1.
Stand tall, take a deep breath (yes, again) and shake off any residual wobble from your time on the throne. You're grounded. You're centred. You've already conquered one mini-battle today – now let's win the war of walking.

2.
Imagine you're wearing a cape. Not an actual one, of course, but a metaphorical one. Hold your head high. Your back is straight. You are a leader. A champion. Someone who can tackle emails like it's a mild inconvenience.

3.
Take your first step – purposeful. Move with the grace of someone who knows exactly where they're going. Even if that's just the kitchen.

4.
As you walk, visualize your energy expanding outward, each step sending waves of calm confidence into the world, like a human-sized ripple in a sea of chaos.

5.
With each step, remind yourself: you've got this. You've had worse. And no, you don't need to check your phone right now.

Optional Mantra:

"I walk like I'm heading toward my destiny and maybe a slightly better cup of coffee."

Note
The power walk is a mind trick, so don't worry if you still look like you're heading to the post office. Confidence is internal. It's the thought that counts.

The Wisdom of Toilet Paper

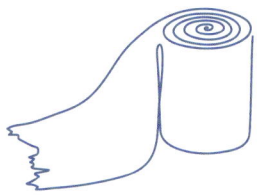

In our exploration of release, we've examined the profound act of letting go. But what of the quiet strength that sustains us in times of need?

Toilet paper, though often dismissed as a mere convenience, is a powerful symbol of life's delicate balance – its humility, its resilience and its ultimate transformation. Let us consider the layers, not just of paper, but of our own lives.

The First Layer

At the beginning of any journey, we stand before
life untouched – untarnished by experience,
unmarked by the weight of the world.

The first layer of toilet paper mirrors this pure,
hopeful state: fresh, open and prepared for
whatever may come.

There is a beauty in this innocence, a promise
that anything is possible. In this moment,
we are ready to face the world with
open arms and a clean slate.

The Middle Layers

As we move forward, life inevitably becomes more complex. Like the middle layers of the roll, we encounter mess, uncertainty and obstacles.

Yet, it is here that our strength truly reveals itself. With each challenge, we grow in resilience, just as the roll of toilet paper unfolds layer by layer to offer greater support.

The journey may get a little "sticky", but the deeper we go, the more we understand that we have the fortitude to endure. The mess is but a temporary part of the process – one that deepens our character and our ability to navigate life's twists and turns.

The Final Layer

And so, we come to the end. The last layer. It arrives swiftly, as endings often do. We may find ourselves facing a moment of transition, unsure of what's next. The final layer serves as a reminder of the cyclical nature of life: every end is but the beginning of something new. And though the roll may seem exhausted, there is always another, ready to take its place. This is the art of renewal, the quiet knowing that life is never truly "finished" – it is merely waiting for the next chapter to unfold.

The Bathroom Manifesto

Write down three things you are ready to release
in your life – whether they be
physical, emotional or mental.

Then imagine yourself flushing them away,
symbolizing the freedom that
comes with letting go.

Place the manifesto somewhere you'll see it
every day as a reminder to carry this
new lightness into the world.

The Golden Flush Challenge

For one week, every time you sit down, take a moment to release a negative thought, frustration or worry as you would a bowel movement.

Let it go, visualize it swirling away and see how much lighter you feel afterward.

Document any noticeable changes in your mood, productivity or outlook.

Conclusion

Wisdom of the Throne

You came seeking relief.
What you found was revelation.

Through breath, stillness, gentle hinges and great releases, you've learned what the sages always knew: that true transformation doesn't roar – it rumbles quietly, from deep within.

And now, as you rise from your porcelain throne, know this: what happens in the bathroom doesn't have to stay in the bathroom.

Take your newfound lightness into the world.

For this is not the end. It's merely the flush before the next beginning.